Betty West
04-17-2016

SEA-SATIONAL

BY ALLYSON KULAVIS

downtown bookworks

downtown bookworks

SPECIAL THANKS: Dr. Andrew Alverson, University of Arkansas; Ann Bauer, The Marine Mammal Center; Dr. John F. Bruno, University of North Carolina at Chapel Hill; Dr. Breea Govenar, Rhode Island College; Dr. Rolf Gradinger, University of Alaska Fairbanks; Dr. Sönke Johnsen, Duke University; Dr. Douglas J. Long, Oakland Museum of California; Dr. Christopher G. Lowe, California State University Long Beach; Dr. Yannis Papastamatiou, Florida Museum of Natural History; Dr. David L. Pawson, National Museum of Natural History, Smithsonian Institution; Dr. Sandra E. Shumway, University of Connecticut; Stefan Wiswedel, Project Seahorse.

Designed by Georgia Rucker
Typeset in Bryant Pro and Warugaki

PHOTO CREDITS Front Cover: Lavigne Herve/Shutterstock.com. 1: NatureDiver/Shutterstock.com. 3: Wim Claes/Shutterstock.com (seal), Ingvars Birznieks/Shutterstock.com (nudibranch). 4–5: tadekz/Shutterstock.com. 4: Ekaterina Pokrovsky/Shutterstock.com (lugworms), cbpix/Shutterstock.com (shark). 5: Kjersti Joergensen/Shutterstock.com. 6: Vilainecrevette/Shutterstock.com. 7: prasit chansareekorn/Shutterstock.com (mantis shrimp), Cigdem Sean Cooper/Shutterstock.com (starry pufferfish), ©Dave Forcucci/SeaPics.com (lanternfish), Photo by Hidden Ocean 2005 Expedition/NOAA Office of Ocean Exploration (deep-sea jellyfish), Photo by NOAA Okeanos Explorer Program, INDEX-SATAL 2010, NOAA/OER (tripodfish), ©Mark V. Erdmann/SeaPics.com (coelacanth). 8: Rich Carey/Shutterstock.com (cuttlefish), Brian Lasenby/Shutterstock.com (tulip snail), ©Pixtal/SuperStock (living mussels), photo-oasis/Shutterstock.com (cooked mussels). 9: JonMilnes/Shutterstock.com. 10: ©Masa Ushioda/SeaPics.com. 11: David Evison/Shutterstock.com (octopus in shell), ©Minden Pictures/SuperStock (octopus ink), Rich Carey/Shutterstock.com (reef octopus), ©Norbert Wu/Science Faction/SuperStock (mimic octopus). 12: Dray van Beeck/Shutterstock.com. 13: Cigdem Sean Cooper/Shutterstock.com (nudibranch grazing), NatureDiver/Shutterstock.com (white nudibranch), cbpix/Shutterstock.com (spotted nudibranch), John A. Anderson/Shutterstock.com (two nudibranchs), stockpix4u/Shutterstock.com (nudibranch laying eggs). 14: orlandin/Shutterstock.com (sea star top), ©Minden Pictures/SuperStock (sea star bottom). 15: Dimitrios/Shutterstock.com (sea urchin tests), NatureDiver/Shutterstock.com (sea urchin), Andrey Nosik/Shutterstock.com (sea cucumber), ©Norbert Wu/Science Faction/SuperStock (sea cucumber shooting threads). 16: Ethan Daniels/Shutterstock.com (lobster), Bennyartist/Shutterstock.com (hinge-beak shrimp), Dana's Destinations/Shutterstock.com (goose barnacles). 17: Tony Florio/Science Source (blue crab), ©Minden Pictures/SuperStock (spider crab). 18: DJ Mattaar/Shutterstock.com (school of fish), ACEgan/Shutterstock.com (jawfish eggs). 19: Sergey Goruppa/Shutterstock.com (catfish), Daniel Petrescu/Shutterstock.com (catfish gills), Stubblefield Photography/Shutterstock.com (hairy frogfish), Khoroshunova Olga/Shutterstock.com (boxfish). 20: Stephan Kerkhofs/Shutterstock.com (ray top corner), Krzysztof Odziomek/Shutterstock.com (manta ray), Sergey Khachatryan/Shutterstock.com (ray's eyes). 21: Konoka Amane/Shutterstock.com (ray underside), ©Shaun Wilkinson/123rf.com (sawfish), Ozger Aybike Sarikaya/Shutterstock.com (ray skin). 22: bluehand/Shutterstock.com. 23: ©Visarute Angkatavanich/123rf.com (red seahorse), ©NaturePL/SuperStock (male giving birth), Jung Hsuan/Shutterstock.com (pygmy seahorses). 24: Vlad61/Shutterstock.com (sea jelly with fish), Dwight Smith/Shutterstock.com (Australian spotted jellyfish). 25: Vilainecrevette/Shutterstock.com (sea jelly tentacles), ©NHPA/SuperStock (stalked jellyfish). 26: Dray van Beeck/Shutterstock.com (dugong), Kirsten Wahlquist/Shutterstock.com (sea otter), BMJ/Shutterstock.com (walruses). 27: Monika Wieland/Shutterstock.com (killer whale), John Tunney/Shutterstock.com (humpback baleen), Cedric Weber/Shutterstock.com (beluga whale), ©BlueGreen Pictures/SuperStock (blue whale). 28: Rich Carey/Shutterstock.com (seagrass), tubuceo/Shutterstock.com (red algae), olmarmar/Shutterstock.com (green algae with feet), Ramon Espelt Photography/Shutterstock.com (green algae). 29: ©FLPA/SuperStock (plankton with phytoplankton), imageZebra/Shutterstock.com (giant kelp). 30: JonMilnes/Shutterstock.com (Christmas tree worms), ©Doug Perrine/SeaPics.com (sea lily). 31: Mark Aplet/Shutterstock.com (sea anemone top), Jiri Vaclavek/Shutterstock.com (sea anemone center), totophotos/Shutterstock.com (sea anemone bottom). 32: Natursports/Shutterstock.com (coral reef top), Photo by G. P. Schmahl NOAA FGBNMS Manager (coral polyps), stephan kerkhofs/Shutterstock.com (coral reef bottom, coral reef bottom close-up). 33: Pinosub/Shutterstock.com. 34: ©age fotostock/SuperStock. 35: Michelle Valberg/All Canada Photos/SuperStock (narwhals), ©Minden Pictures/SuperStock (isopod with sea stars, Antarctic icefish). 36: ©Minden Pictures/SuperStock (black swallower), Joe Belanger/Shutterstock.com (sea cucumber), zimmytws/Shutterstock.com (pelican). 37: ©Doug Perrine/SeaPics.com (dolphins), peter herbig/Photos.com (sea star), Tyler Fox/Shutterstock.com (coral polyp). 38: ©Doug Perrine/SeaPics.com. 39: ©Tobias Friedrich/F1 ONLINE/SuperStock (bobtail squid), Jupiterimages/Photos.com (comb jelly). 40: ©NaturePL/SuperStock. 41: ©Minden Pictures/SuperStock (both). 42: ©Susan Dabritz/SeaPics.com (vent dandelion, deep-sea worm), Photo by OAR/National Undersea Research Program (NURP)/NOAA (hydrothermal vent). 43: ©Susan Dabritz/SeaPics.com. 44: Krzysztof Odziomek/Shutterstock.com (lionfish), Cigdem Sean Cooper/Shutterstock.com (stonefish). 45: Ernie Hounshell/Shutterstock.com (inflated pufferfish), Elisei Shafer/Shutterstock.com (deflated pufferfish). 46: BMJ/Shutterstock.com (fish in net), Vladimir Melnik/Shutterstock.com (polar bear). 47: KN/Shutterstock.com (chemicals), Sam Chadwick/Shutterstock.com (trash), Ilya D. Gridnev/Shutterstock.com (sea star with many arms), Kulish Viktoriia/Shutterstock.com (sea star top left), Andrew Chin/Shutterstock.com (small brown sea star), bddigitalimages/Shutterstock.com (sand dollar test), Erica Kyte/Fotolia.com (live sand dollars). Back Cover: Sergey Khachatryan/Shutterstock.com (ray), totophotos/Shutterstock.com (clownfish and sea anemone).

Printed in China, March 2013
ISBN 978-1-935703-55-6
10 9 8 7 6 5 4 3 2 1
Downtown Bookworks Inc.
285 West Broadway
New York, NY 10013
www.dtbwpub.com

CONTENTS

4	Hello, Is There Anybody Out There?
6	From Light to Dark
8	Marvelous Mollusks
10	Outrageous Octopuses!
12	What Is a Nudibranch?
14	Spiny, Spiky, Crawly
16	Armor-Plated Animals
18	Fascinating Fish
20	Ocean Gliders
22	The Seahorse, of Course
24	Sea Jellies
26	Marine Mammals
28	Algae and Sea Plants
30	Plant or Animal?
32	Coral Reefs
34	Cold-Water Critters
36	Dinnertime!
38	Let It Glow!
40	Creatures of the Deep
42	Underwater Hot Spots
44	Catch Me if You Dare!
46	Oceans in Trouble
48	Superstars of the Sea

HELLO,
IS THERE ANYBODY OUT THERE?

Our oceans and seas are filled with life. In fact, most of the Earth's living things are found in and around the water. Aside from fish, there are sea birds (like albatross and penguins), reptiles (like sea snakes and turtles), mammals (like seals and whales), invertebrates (like squid and sponges), and many, many different kinds of plants and algae (like seagrass and seaweed).

Blacktip reef shark

Lugworms eat sand, digest anything edible, and then poop out the leftover sand, leaving little piles near their burrows.

Most plants and animals prefer to live near sunlight and warmth, so the waters closest to the surface are where most sea life is found. Many animals also live on the sandy shores near the coast. They survive by burrowing, or digging, into the sand or mud.

Some areas of the ocean support very little sea life. Few plants and animals can survive in very hot or freezing cold waters.

Hawksbill sea turtle

FROM LIGHT TO DARK

Scientists divide the ocean into layers, or zones. The deeper the water, the darker and colder it is. The pressure also increases with the added weight of all the water above.

SUNLIT OR PHOTIC ZONE

0 to 660 feet down (0 to 201 m)

There's enough light in this zone for plants and algae to make their own food using sunlight through the process of photosynthesis. About 90% of all marine life lives in this zone.

TWILIGHT ZONE 660 to 3,300 feet down (201 to 1,006 m)

It's too dark in the twilight zone for plants to grow. As the amount of sunlight in an area decreases, animals' eyes get bigger. There is just enough light to hunt by. Only a few deep-diving mammals, such as elephant seals and sperm whales can cope with the increasing pressure in this zone. Some animals in this zone create their own light or move up into the sunlit zone to feed at night.

DARK AND ABYSSAL ZONES 3,300 to 36,300 feet down (1,006 to 11,064 m)

Pressure in the dark zone is more than 100 times that of the surface. That's enough pressure to crush the lungs of a human. Eyes are not very useful in this near-freezing darkness. Some animals in this zone have long sensory hairs and feelers that help them get around and find food. Having a huge mouth also makes it easier to grab food. Many animals here eat sinking debris known as "marine snow."

Mantis shrimp

Starry
pufferfish

Lanternfish

Coelacanth
(*seel*-uh-canth)

More than 90%
of all water in the
ocean is dark and
below 43°F (6°C).

Tripodfish

Deep-sea jellyfish

MARVELOUS MOLLUSKS

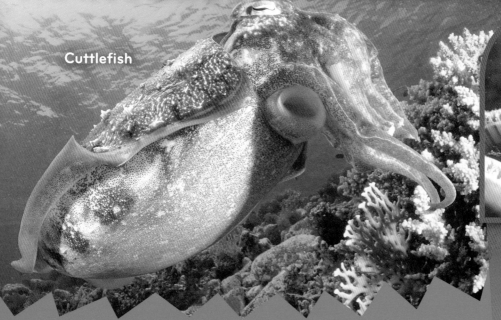

Cuttlefish

Living mussels look different from the ones you'll find on a dinner plate.

Cuttlefish and clams may not look alike, but they are related. They are both soft-bodied creatures called **mollusks.** Other animals in this group are oysters, conchs, slugs, and snails. Many of them have a shell to protect their squishy body. Cuttlefish, squid, and octopuses do not have shells, but they do have tentacles and a sharp, powerful mouth like the beak of a hawk.
All mollusks have a head, a body, and a foot. Their foot does not look anything like a human foot, but it helps them move around.

Mollusks with two shells are called bivalves.

The foot of a tulip snail

The giant clam is the largest bivalve in the world. It stays in one spot its entire life, growing up to 4 feet (1.2 m) wide. That's probably wider than you are tall!

Scientists have recently discovered clams that secrete an antibiotic. They hope that one day we may be able to use this as medicine.

OUTRAGEOUS OCTOPUSES!

Invertebrates are animals with no backbone, and the oceans are filled with them. Octopuses have the largest brain of all invertebrates. Unlike a human brain, octopus brains extend throughout their entire body. More than half of an octopus's brain is in its arms!

Octopuses have eight incredibly strong arms that are covered with suckers. Each arm and sucker can move on its own. This allows octopuses incredibly precise movement.

New evidence suggests that octopuses can actually see with their skin!

Octopuses can taste with their suckers!

At the center of its body is an octopus's mouth. It has a beak similar to the beak of a parrot, which it uses to pry open crab shells. Then it will use its radula, or barbed tongue, to scrape the crab out of its shell. If this doesn't work, an octopus has a mouthpart that can actually drill through the shells of other animals.

Octopuses can squeeze into teeny, tiny places.

Octopuses squirt ink at predators and then quickly swim away without being seen.

This reef octopus is a master of blending into its surroundings.

All octopuses can change their appearance, but the mimic octopus will also imitate the movements of other animals, such as sea jellies and sea anemones. To look like a banded sea snake, the mimic octopus might bury six of its legs in the sand and stretch out the other two.

This mimic octopus looks and acts like a sand-dwelling flounder.

11

WHAT IS A NUDIBRANCH?

Like squids and octopuses, nudibranchs are mollusks that do not have shells as adults. Often found in shallow, tropical waters, nudibranchs can be as small as 0.25 inches (0.6 cm) and up to 12 inches (30 cm) long. There are more than 3,000 known species of nudibranchs, and new ones are identified almost daily. Nudibranchs are meat-eaters. They often feed on sponges, anemones, corals, and barnacles. They even eat other nudibranchs. Some ooze poison from their skin after eating poisonous animals.

Some nudibranchs are solar powered. They store cells from the algae they eat in the outer layers of their skin. These cells react with the sun to produce sugars that the nudibranch eats. This process, called photosynthesis, is how plants make their own food with the help of the sun.

A nudibranch grazing on algae and coral

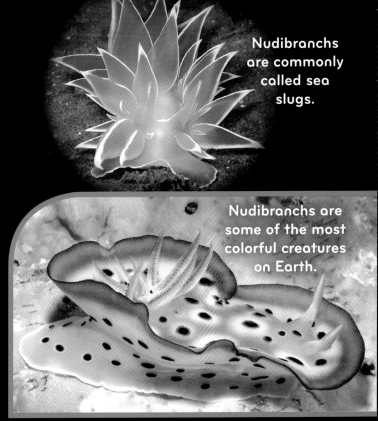

Nudibranchs are commonly called sea slugs.

Nudibranchs are some of the most colorful creatures on Earth.

Many nudibranchs lay eggs that look like ribbons.

Bright colors usually indicate that an animal is poisonous, so scientists believe a nudibranch's appearance helps to discourage other animals from eating it.

13

SPINY, SPIKY, CRAWLY

Spiny sea stars, spiky sea urchins, and crawly sea cucumbers, are all members of a group of animals called echinoderms (ih-*ky*-nuh-durms). Scientists have discovered about 7,000 different species of echinoderms throughout the ocean, from shallow tropical shores to the greatest ocean depths.

Sea stars have spines covering their backs as protection, and many tube feet on their underside to help them get around. They do not swim, but the fastest sea stars can move quickly, almost 10 feet (3 m) in a minute.

Sea urchins are covered in sharp spikes, and some spikes have venom in their tips. Still, the birds, otters, crabs, and other animals

The bottom of a sea star is covered with tube feet.

The most remarkable thing about all echinoderms is their ability to regenerate, or grow back, an organ or limb. In some cases, an entire animal can regenerate from a single limb.

Sea urchin spikes fall off when they die, leaving beautiful shells called tests.

Sea urchin

that eat sea urchins have found ways to get to the urchin's soft body. Sea urchins have five strong teeth on their underside for eating. These teeth are strong enough to bore a hole in a rock to make a hiding place for the urchin.

Some sea cucumbers have bumpy, leathery skin. Others look an awful lot like actual cucumbers. Like underwater vacuum cleaners, sea cucumbers scoop up mud and sand to eat.

To distract potential predators, some sea cucumbers, like the one below, can shoot long sticky threads from their bodies. Others can discharge their internal organs. Don't worry, their guts grow back.

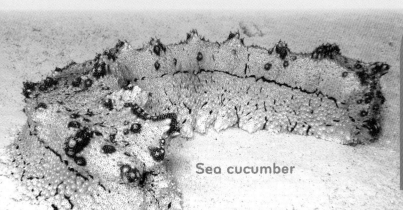

Sea cucumber

ARMOR-PLATED ANIMALS

Crabs, shrimp, lobsters, and barnacles are all crustaceans. Most crustaceans live in the water. Some crustaceans stay put and others move around. But they all have one thing in common: a hard external skeleton called an exoskeleton. These armor-plated creatures are related to insects, spiders, and scorpions.

Many crabs and shrimp can swim, but lobsters usually only scuttle along the sea floor.

The hinge-beak shrimp is also known as the camel shrimp or the dancing shrimp.

Goose barnacles remain in one place, usually attached to a rock, for their entire adult life.

As crustaceans grow, they must molt, or shed their exoskeleton. They break out of an exoskeleton once it becomes too small for their body. After they molt, the outside layer of their skin hardens and becomes a new, larger exoskeleton.

In order for it to molt, a crab's shell will split open in the back. Here, a blue crab backs out of its hard exoskeleton.

After a lobster molts, it will often eat its old shell. Crabs don't. That's why you'll find many more old crab shells washed up on the beach.

A spider crab (on the right) stands next to its discarded exoskeleton.

FASCINATING FISH

Scientists have found more than 25,000 kinds of fish. Scientists think there may be tens of thousands more that have yet to be discovered. Each one has its own habits.

Sometimes fish swim together in shoals or schools. Shoaling fish stick together, but they may not be doing the exact same things as their neighbors. Schooling fish move in tight patterns. These fish formations can confuse predators. Swimming in groups also helps fish to find mates.

When a female jawfish lays her eggs, the male scoops them up in his mouth to protect them. He will not eat for 7 to 9 days, so the eggs can hatch and the babies can swim away.

Fish can't breathe air, but they do need oxygen to survive. Luckily, oxygen is a gas that can dissolve in water. All fish have special, feathery organs called gills. Gills pull oxygen from the water and move it into the animal's blood stream. If a fish is in water with very little oxygen, the fish can't survive. This is why fish tanks have pumps that bubble oxygen into the water. Pollution can decrease the amount of oxygen in water, making it dangerous for fish.

Catfish gills

Many fish have scales that overlap all over the body, creating a tough, flexible layer of protection. A boxfish's scales are different. They are more like bony plates that are fused together, giving these fish their boxlike appearance. When a boxfish is in danger, it can release poison into the water.

Instead of swimming, hairy frogfishes "walk" on their pectoral fins (the ones right behind the head). They can also fill up with water. When they push the water out of their body, they shoot in the opposite direction. This kind of jet propulsion helps them get around more quickly.

OCEAN GLIDERS

Like a shark, a ray is a cartilaginous (kar-til-*aj*-ih-nuss) fish. That's because their skeletons are made of flexible cartilage instead of bone. Bend your nose or ear. They are made of cartilage too. Cartilaginous fish have tough, toothlike scales that cover and protect their skin. Rays are sometimes killed for their skin and meat.

Rays do not lay eggs. Their young are born alive. Skates, which are similar to rays, give birth to eggs in an egg case.

Manta rays are the world's biggest rays. They can grow to be almost 30 feet (9 m) across! They are filter feeders. They pull water into their mouth to catch any plankton (see page 29) or small fish that might be in the water. These graceful animals are harmless to humans.

Close-up of ray skin

Some rays ripple their body in a wavelike motion to glide through the water. Others flap their sides like wings to swim. The flattened body of a ray also helps many rays hide and hunt on the ocean floor. Most rays have flat teeth that can crush the hard shells of crustaceans and mollusks.

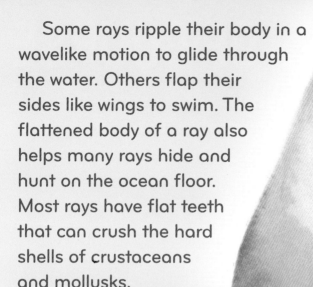

A ray's mouth, nostrils, and gills are on the underside of their body.

Sawfish are rays with long, flat, sawlike snouts. They use their snouts to slash through groups of fish or to dig for shellfish.

Sawfish are in danger of becoming extinct.

A ray's eyes are on the topside of their body.

The tip of a blue-spotted stingray's tail is covered with a venomous mucus. The venom will not kill a human, but it sure can hurt.

THE SEAHORSE, OF COURSE

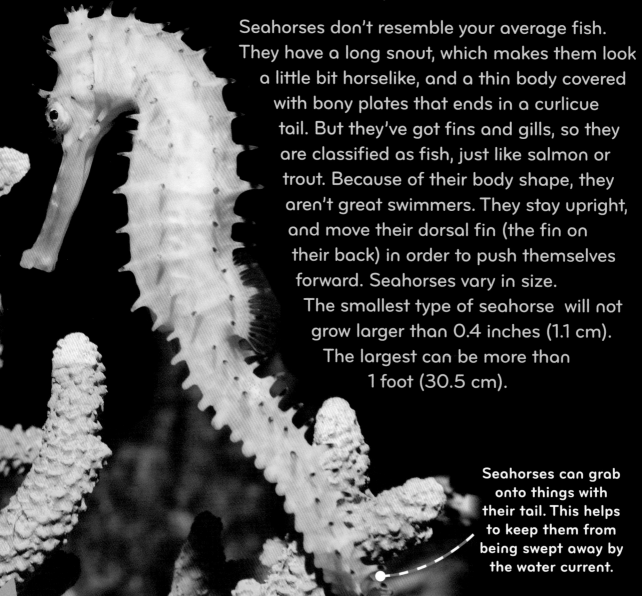

Seahorses don't resemble your average fish. They have a long snout, which makes them look a little bit horselike, and a thin body covered with bony plates that ends in a curlicue tail. But they've got fins and gills, so they are classified as fish, just like salmon or trout. Because of their body shape, they aren't great swimmers. They stay upright, and move their dorsal fin (the fin on their back) in order to push themselves forward. Seahorses vary in size. The smallest type of seahorse will not grow larger than 0.4 inches (1.1 cm). The largest can be more than 1 foot (30.5 cm).

Seahorses can grab onto things with their tail. This helps to keep them from being swept away by the water current.

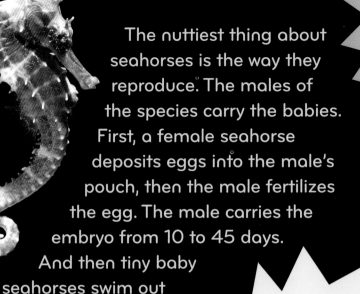

The nuttiest thing about seahorses is the way they reproduce. The males of the species carry the babies. First, a female seahorse deposits eggs into the male's pouch, then the male fertilizes the egg. The male carries the embryo from 10 to 45 days.

And then tiny baby seahorses swim out of their dad's pouch. These creatures choose one mate and stay together for the season or for the rest of their lives.

At the very top of a seahorse's head is a bony ridge called a coronet. Each one is unique. Much like we use fingerprints to identify people, scientists use coronets to tell one seahorse from another.

The temperature of the water a seahorse lives in affects how long a male seahorse will be pregnant. The hotter the water, the shorter the pregnancy is.

A pregnant male seahorse gives birth.

To stay safe, tiny pygmy seahorses look just like the plant or animal that they call home. Can you spot the seahorses in the photo?

23

SEA JELLIES

Some fish are not affected by sea jelly stings. They can swim around sea jelly tentacles for protection.

Sea jellies are often called jellyfish, but they are not fish at all. They have no bones, brains, hearts, complex eyes, or respiratory system (for breathing). They are made almost entirely of water, and they have floated in the ocean since before dinosaurs walked on Earth.

Jellies can be found in every ocean on the planet. They can live in the deepest parts of the ocean or float

Australian spotted jellyfish

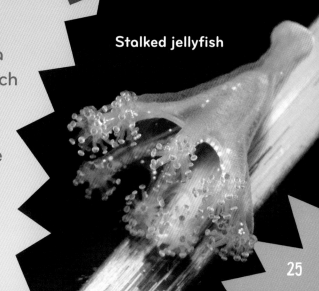

Many sea jellies are almost completely see-through. Others are more colorful. Some jellies even light up like electric signs!

A group of jellies is called a smack.

Long, stinging tentacles trail from the body of most jellies. Any animal that gets caught in the sticky, venomous tentacles can become the jelly's next meal. The tentacles of some jellies can grow longer than 100 feet (30.5 m).

Stalked jellyfish

close to the surface of the water. Most live close to land in either harbors or bays. Some even live in freshwater. Sea jellies can range from smaller than 1 inch (2.5 cm) to several feet across in size.

Most jellies float and drift on the currents of the ocean. Some also move up and down in the water by pulsing their bodies. Stalked jellyfish spend their entire lives attached to seaweed or seagrass.

25

MARINE MAMMALS

Dugongs like this one are herbivores. They eat only plants. Manatees are herbivorous sea creatures, too.

All mammals breathe air. Mammals that live in the ocean must return to the surface to fill their lungs with air. Even though they aren't furry as adults, dolphins, porpoises, and whales are mammals. Seals, sea lions, and walruses are furry sea mammals.

As far as we know, blue whales are the largest animals to have ever lived on the planet.

The smallest sea mammal is the sea otter.

Walruses use their tusks for fighting, to attract a mate, and to pull themselves up onto the ice.

These graceful giants can be 100 feet (30 m) long, and yet their main diet is a tiny shrimp-like animal called krill. The mouth plate of a blue whale is covered with a hairlike structure called baleen. The whales take a huge amount of water into their mouth, and the baleen helps to filter out the krill.

Bowhead, blue, humpback, fin, and gray whales are all baleen whales. Beluga and pilot whales are types of whales with teeth.

Killer whales are actually the largest members of the dolphin family.

The shaggy baleen helps this whale to filter food from the ocean water.

Blue whales are believed to be the loudest animals on the planet. They also have excellent hearing and can communicate with one another from 1,000 miles (1,609 km) away.

Beluga whales live in cold Arctic waters.

A blue whale can eat about 4 tons (3.6 metric tons) of krill in a single day. That would be like eating 16,000 plates of spaghetti every 24 hours.

ALGAE AND SEA PLANTS

The largest plantlike organisms in the ocean are seaweeds. Seaweeds are not actually weeds or even plants, but something called *algae*. Some of the biggest are giant kelp. They can grow 17 inches (13 cm) in a day, reaching incredible lengths of 82 to 164 feet (25 to 50 m) in a season! They form thick underwater "forests" that are home to many different animals.

Ocean plants, such as seagrass, and most types of algae convert sunlight and nutrients in the water into food for themselves. In the process, they create the oxygen that marine animals breathe. They also provide a rich source of food for many creatures in the sea.

Red algae

Seagrass

Brown algae

Certain kinds of seaweed are used to make ice cream, toothpaste, candy bars, and salad dressing. If you see *carrageenan* in the list of ingredients, you are eating red seaweed.

Green algae

Using a microscope, scientists can see plankton and phytoplankton, like the diatoms pictured here.

Giant kelp

There are tiny plants and animals known as **plankton** drifting in the sea. They are smaller than the dot on this i. More than 90% of living things in the sea are plankton. Many small animals eat plankton. Then larger animals eat the smaller ones. Just about every creature in the ocean relies on plankton (or the animals that eat plankton) for food. Plantlike plankton are called **phytoplankton** (*fie*-toh-plank-tun).

Phytoplankton are major oxygen producers. About a third of the oxygen you breathe comes from phytoplankton.

PLANT OR ANIMAL?

Some creatures under the sea look a lot like brightly colored plants from outer space. But they actually belong to the animal kingdom. Instead of actively hunting for food, they often stay fixed to one spot and wait for food to float, crawl, or swim close by.

Christmas tree worms burrow holes into coral. The parts sticking out help the worm to breathe and eat. Curious critters get trapped in these furry "crowns" and become a meal for the worm.

A sea lily uses its feathery arms to filter food from the water.

Most sea anemones spend their entire life attached to a single rock. Some latch on to hermit crabs. Anemones are found all over the world in both cold and warm waters. Their tentacles have venomous stingers, so they can trap and stun an animal or tiny organism before pulling it into their mouth.

This anemone looks like a desert cactus flower.

Clownfish are one of the few animals that are not bothered by anemone stings. So they live in anemones, where they are protected from other animals.

31

CORAL REEFS

A coral reef is formed from the stony skeletons of tiny animals called coral polyps. Coral polyps are fascinating. They reproduce in two different ways.

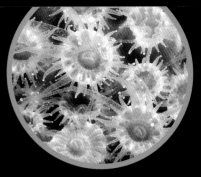

Coral polyps

• The female releases the eggs into the water, and the male fertilizes them. Tiny larvae hatch from the eggs and drift in the water. Soon they land on hard surfaces, such as rocks, and attach themselves. The larvae grow into polyps. Their bodies are like small bags with tentacles at one end for catching prey (see page 37).

• Coral polyps can also reproduce by splitting in half. They divide again and again until there is an entire colony of polyps.

Scientists predict that many coral reefs will be lost within our lifetime. One threat comes from carbon dioxide (CO_2), which is released when we burn oil and coal. The CO_2 gets into the water, making it more acidic. This acidification harms animals (see page 46).

Algae, sponges, anemones, nudibranchs, worms, eels, barnacles, and many fish live in and around coral reefs. Coral reefs can be hundreds, even thousands of years old. Most are found in warm tropical waters, but scientists are also exploring cold, deepwater coral reefs. Aside from providing a home to many sea creatures and plants, coral can also protect coasts. A large coral reef will slow down powerful ocean waves before they crash into the shore and damage the coastline.

A patch of Australia's Great Barrier Reef has more living things in it than an equal-size patch of a tropical rain forest.

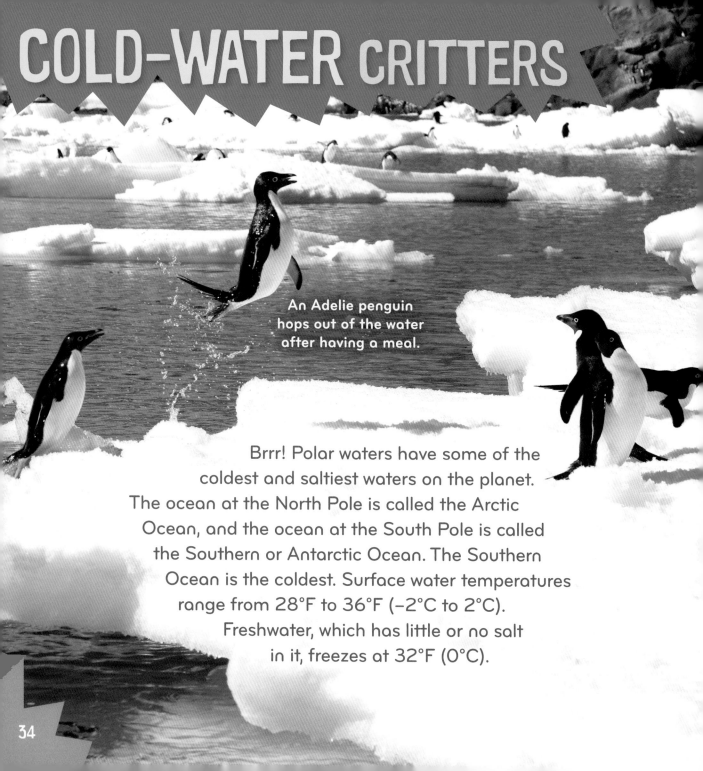

COLD-WATER CRITTERS

An Adelie penguin hops out of the water after having a meal.

Brrr! Polar waters have some of the coldest and saltiest waters on the planet. The ocean at the North Pole is called the Arctic Ocean, and the ocean at the South Pole is called the Southern or Antarctic Ocean. The Southern Ocean is the coldest. Surface water temperatures range from 28°F to 36°F (–2°C to 2°C). Freshwater, which has little or no salt in it, freezes at 32°F (0°C).

Narwhals live only in the Arctic Ocean. The males have hornlike spiral tusks that can grow up to 10 feet (3 m) long!

A giant isopod and sea stars deep in Antarctic waters

Enormous blue whales, giant squids, and Antarctic anemones are just a few of the animals that live in these chilly waters. The killer whale, or orca, is the top marine predator in both the Southern and Arctic Oceans. They often hunt in groups or pods.

The Antarctic icefish and the bald notothen (pictured here living in an iceberg) have antifreeze in their blood to keep them from freezing.

35

DINNERTIME!

There are about as many ways to find and eat food in the ocean as there are animals doing the eating. Each of these animals has its own special way of enjoying a meal.

The deep-sea-dwelling black swallower has a huge stomach and can eat a fish three times its size.

Sea cucumbers have tube feet around their mouth to help them scoop up food.

Pelicans dive into the water and use the pouch in their beak to scoop up fish. They then drain the water from the pouch and swallow whatever food they captured.

One way dolphins feed is called herding. Working together in groups, or pods, dolphins will herd a group of fish together in a tight ball, known as a bait ball. Then the dolphins will take turns swimming through the ball and eating as many fish as possible.

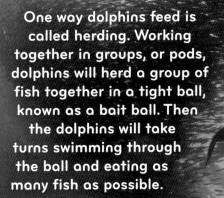

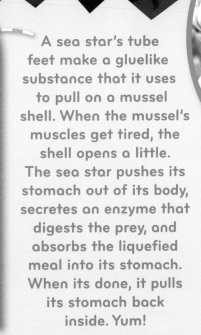

A sea star's tube feet make a gluelike substance that it uses to pull on a mussel shell. When the mussel's muscles get tired, the shell opens a little. The sea star pushes its stomach out of its body, secretes an enzyme that digests the prey, and absorbs the liquefied meal into its stomach. When its done, it pulls its stomach back inside. Yum!

Coral polyps feed at night. They extend their tentacles, snatching up plankton as it floats by. Like a long sticky tongue, the tentacles draw food into the mouth.

37

LET IT GLOW!

Some amazing animals can use the chemicals or bacteria in their body to make their own light. This ability is called **bioluminescence.** Something glowing in normally pitch-black waters can attract a mate, lure in prey, or scare away an animal looking for a quick meal.

Bioluminescent plankton light up a beach on an island in the Maldives, in the Indian Ocean. When groups of plankton are aglow, any fish (or other predators) around them will be visible, making them the targets of other, larger predators.

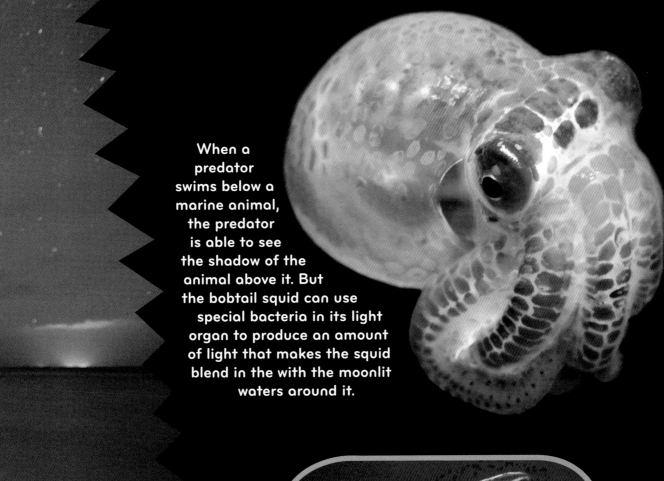

When a predator swims below a marine animal, the predator is able to see the shadow of the animal above it. But the bobtail squid can use special bacteria in its light organ to produce an amount of light that makes the squid blend in the with the moonlit waters around it.

Many comb jellies are bioluminescent.

CREATURES OF **THE DEEP**

In the deepest, darkest areas of the ocean, there is no sunlight and no plant life. Meat-eating animals like the deep-sea anglerfish, hatchetfish, and the giant squid have found ways to survive.

Fish are attracted to the glowing lure perched above the deep-sea anglerfish's head. When an animal comes close, the anglerfish uses its large mouth and sharp teeth to make sure that meal does not get away.

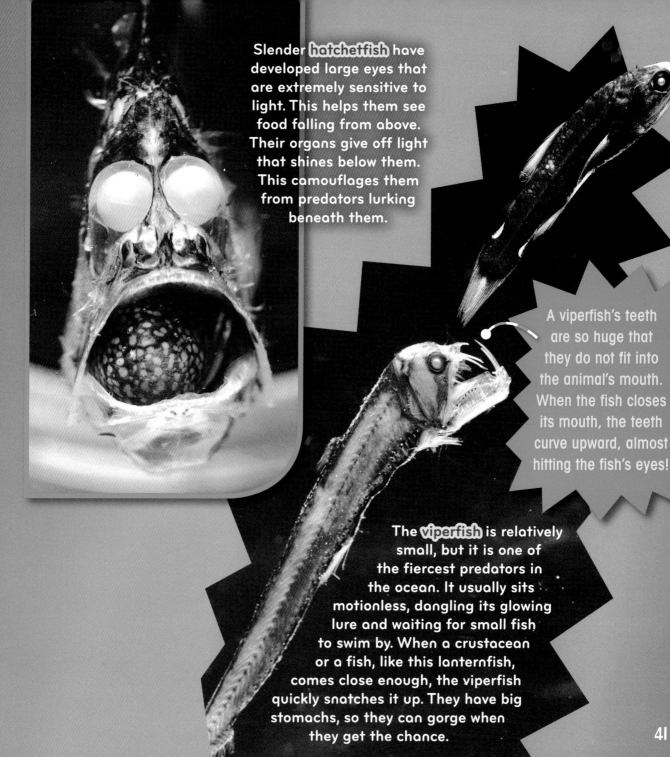

Slender **hatchetfish** have developed large eyes that are extremely sensitive to light. This helps them see food falling from above. Their organs give off light that shines below them. This camouflages them from predators lurking beneath them.

A viperfish's teeth are so huge that they do not fit into the animal's mouth. When the fish closes its mouth, the teeth curve upward, almost hitting the fish's eyes!

The **viperfish** is relatively small, but it is one of the fiercest predators in the ocean. It usually sits motionless, dangling its glowing lure and waiting for small fish to swim by. When a crustacean or a fish, like this lanternfish, comes close enough, the viperfish quickly snatches it up. They have big stomachs, so they can gorge when they get the chance.

UNDERWATER HOT SPOTS

The ocean floor has vast flat plains, huge mountains, active volcanoes, and deep trenches. In some of the lowest points of the ocean, plumes of hot water gush out of the Earth's crust. Known as hydrothermal vents, these water spouts are similar to hot springs on land.

Water around a hydrothermal vent can be as hot as 760°F (404°C). But jets of extremely hot water quickly mix with much cooler seawater, making the areas around the vents kind of like naturally occuring Jacuzzis.

Vent dandelions are related to sea jellies. Each ball is actually hundreds of animals balled together.

The Pompeii worm is found only at hydrothermal vents in the Pacific Ocean.

Before the discovery of hydrothermal vents in 1979, no one expected to find busy colonies of animals living in the cold, dark deep sea. At an average of 7,000 feet (2,134 m), these vents spew out incredibly hot, mineral-rich seawater. The mix of chemicals and heat would be deadly to most organisms, but some creatures, such as eelpout fish, giant tubeworms, Galatheid crabs (also known as squat lobsters), and heat-tolerant mussels, thrive near these vents.

Giant tubeworms wriggle inside of leathery white tubes. Other organisms often live inside the tubes too. The tubeworms have no digestive system. Instead, they survive on internal bacteria that use chemicals rather than sunlight for energy.

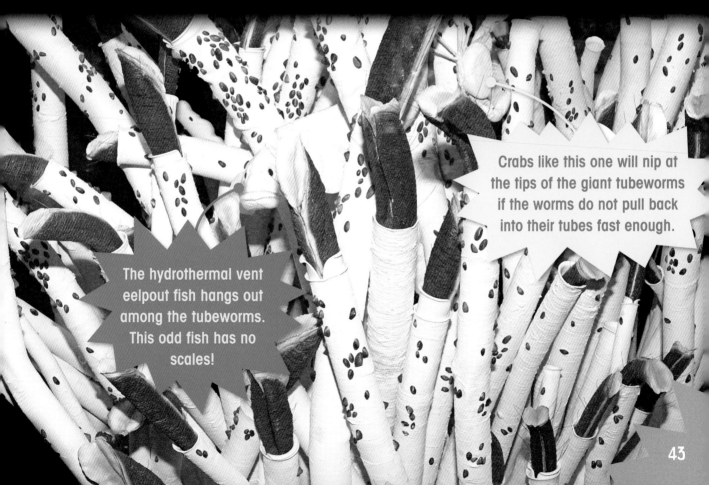

Crabs like this one will nip at the tips of the giant tubeworms if the worms do not pull back into their tubes fast enough.

The hydrothermal vent eelpout fish hangs out among the tubeworms. This odd fish has no scales!

CATCH ME IF YOU DARE!

People have tried to catch or eat almost every kind of animal they've found in the ocean. In the process, they have discovered that many are actually poisonous and extremely dangerous.

The many spines of a lionfish can deliver venom to any animal that comes close. For a human, these stings are incredibly painful and can make breathing difficult, but they are not usually deadly. Some adventurous eaters like to eat lionfish, with the toxic fins removed, of course.

Stonefish have the largest venom glands of any fish. They lie still, looking just like the seafloor around them. A person who accidentally steps on a stonefish can permanently lose feeling in the wounded limb, become paralyzed, or even die.

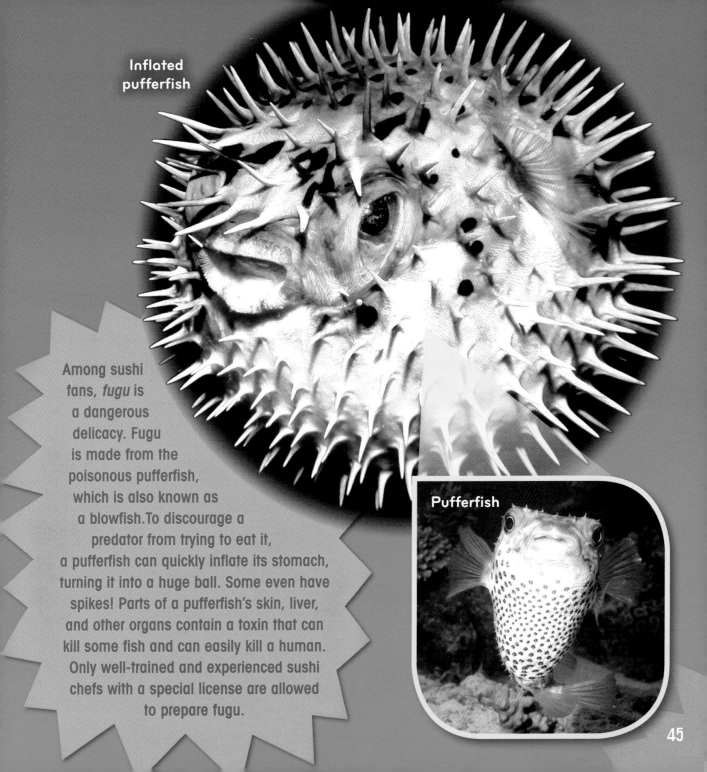

Inflated pufferfish

Among sushi fans, *fugu* is a dangerous delicacy. Fugu is made from the poisonous pufferfish, which is also known as a blowfish. To discourage a predator from trying to eat it, a pufferfish can quickly inflate its stomach, turning it into a huge ball. Some even have spikes! Parts of a pufferfish's skin, liver, and other organs contain a toxin that can kill some fish and can easily kill a human. Only well-trained and experienced sushi chefs with a special license are allowed to prepare fugu.

Pufferfish

45

OCEANS IN TROUBLE

Every few hundred thousand years, Earth goes through natural cycles of cooler and warmer climate conditions. We are in the middle of a warmer cycle, but scientists believe that air pollution is making the planet a lot hotter, a lot faster. Scientists have discovered that burning coal and oil to generate power increases the amount of carbon dioxide in the air. This invisible gas heats up the planet. As temperatures go up, the plants and animals in the oceans suffer.

Humans are also overfishing, removing many of the ocean's large predators. Some fishing boats drag nets that are larger than two football fields across the ocean floor, scooping up everything in their path. Endangered fish, coral, seals, and whales are often killed by these nets.

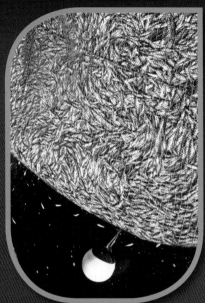

Commercial fishermen are catching more fish than the ocean can replace.

Melting ice causes flooding and robs many animals of a home.

Oceans are being polluted by chemical fertilizers, plastic waste, sewage, and oil spills. Over time, even pesticides sprayed on our lawns can be carried into the ocean by rain. Anything we put into a sewer goes straight into the ocean.

YOU CAN HELP!

We can help save the oceans and the planet. Here are a few things you can do.

- Use less fuel and energy. Take the bus, ride a bike, or walk, instead of riding in a car. Put on a sweater and turn down the heat a few degrees.

- Make less trash. Reuse containers and bags. Recycle instead of throwing things in the trash.

- Do not put hazardous chemicals in the regular trash. Medicine, paint, cleaning fluids, oil, and insect sprays should never go down the sink or toilet. Use nontoxic products to clean your clothes, dishes, and bodies.

- Be an activist. Learn more and share your knowledge with others.

SUPERSTARS OF THE SEA

A sea stars's mouth is in the center of the underside of its body.

Sea stars are found all over the world, in busy tropical waters and in the cold depths of the sea. Most sea stars, like the one that comes with this book, have five arms. If there is a major difference in the size of the arms on your sea star, it may be because your sea star has regrown one or more of its limbs.

Some sea stars have many arms.

Look closely at the tip of each arm of your sea star. That's where the animal's eyes are. They don't see like people do, but they can detect changes in light.

Like sea stars, sand dollars are echinoderms (see page 14). When they're alive, sand dollars are covered with short spines, which are used to burrow and to pass food along their bodies to their mouths.

In calm water, sand dollars stand up on their sides, stuck in the sand. When the water is rough, they lie flat and bury themselves.

Notice the star shape on the back of your sand dollar test. The animal's mouth is in the center of that star, on the underside of its body.

48